COME THE DE

COME THE DEEP WATER

*for Richard
with best wishes*

H. H. Batory

od 87

by

Elizabeth Batory

TABB HOUSE

First published 1987
Tabb House, 11 Church Street, Padstow, Cornwall.

British Library Cataloguing in Publication Data
    Batory, Elizabeth
       Come the deep water: sea stories.
       I. Title
       823'.914 [F]   PS6052.A7/
       ISBN 0-907018-56-4

Typeset by St George Typesetting
Redruth, Cornwall.

Printed by A. Wheaton & Co., Ltd.
Exeter, Devon

CONTENTS

COME THE DEEP WATER

THE clouds were banking up in an indigo haze behind the Old Harry rock, as our boat rose and dipped on the rising sea-swell. The orange lines trailed out behind the stern as we span for mackerel. Sometimes luck was with us and when we ran into a shoal we would have the deck flapping with silver fish as the trippers triumphantly pulled in catch after catch. I had skippered the trips all summer long and now the season was drawing to a close; already the visitors were thinning in the town. But it was good while it lasted; free spending and high living, at least for the length of the holidays. Trips round the bay and all aboard the *Skylark* were as popular as ever, and when the weather was fair we were well patronised. I'd a morning job, then, that saw to the most of my expenses, but I preferred my afternoons on the sea; out on the water, my hand on the helm and the surge of the tide beneath my feet.

Old Ned took most of the bookings; I sometimes thought he was our main attraction and advertisement, with his old navy cap, blue Guernsey over his seaman's paunch, his rolling gait and sea-blue eyes, forever set on a distant horizon. I was a lad then and Ned's been dead these twenty years, but we worked well together, understood each other, and prospered in each other's company.

Now as we headed for home and I set the nose of the boat once more back towards the bay, I noticed the white shadow of a flickering, struggling caught mackerel being hauled past me. Too quickly, far too quickly, for with a dart of metal and a flurry of foam it was gone – or appeared to go – but I saw its silver form floating towards the bottom of the sea; and as it did, a strange phenomenon occurred or

1

a distortion of my vision seemed to take place. It was as though the fish had got larger with the depths, its form more sinuous, and its colour whiter.

Boatmen can't take their eyes off the sea for long; the spring tide had ceased ebbing and nearer the rocks of Peveril the breaking waves signalled a stronger flow. A couple of waves hit us broadside on. Having set the boat to rights, I glanced down at the sea again and at the strange fish. It was still there, calmly following the boat, although our speed could only have been as little as a knot. It seemed more to be drifting under the boat with a luminescent whiteness. Glancing up at the sky I could see already rain was falling on the hills inland, although, as often is the case, the bay was bright and sunny. Indeed many of the passengers had their jackets off and were happier sitting sunbathing than paying serious attention to catching fish.

I was disconcerted, but not unduly so. It was just something I couldn't explain. But the sea is full of such things. Once we had to pull a suicide out of the water; but as old Ned remarked "It's not the dead that worry me, it's those that we find in the water that are still alive".

Ned and I, sitting in the Three Feathers that night, drinking away the takings as he put it, decided I'd been fancying things, and having too many late nights and too many beers too often.

But the story was good for a couple of free pints and when I was next in the pub I told the lads the same story. As I turned to hand a jar to one of my mates I saw a girl on a stool by the bar with sea-strange eyes. Not blue and distant with a fair weather haze in them like Ned's and not a sharp sapphire blue like my mother's, but swimming with greys and greens and turquoise.

I hesitated, I was suddenly adrift. Until the bark of lewd laughter, the chink of glasses, and the smell of beer and cigarette smoke broke the spell of sea-magic.

2

Next time out, I didn't know I was looking for her; but next time I saw her, I knew I was looking for her. It took no imagination to make out the slender and undulatory form of her body alongside but deep down beside the boat. This time I didn't tell Ned. After that, sometimes, if it was at all possible, I would take the boat alone out to sea hoping that on my own I would catch a glimpse, a look long enough to put the seal of certainty on what I thought, what I hoped and what I dreaded.

Never; never did I see her on those lone voyages. Summer slowly unstretched and outfurled those long glowing evenings that breathe of autumn. Blackberries had appeared in the hedgerows, the season was drawing to a close, and it would soon be time to draw the boats ashore and beach them for the winter.

There were a last few days left for the ever-hopeful mackerel fishers. We put out on the first trip of the afternoon; a couple of late-comers managed to spring from Ned's boat, which was off to the Smuggler's Caves, into mine. Shipping the fenders, engine full throttle we were out in the harbour, weaving our way through the tiny craft moored there. Come the deep water and the lines paid out, I set to collecting the fares and fastening the slackened lines. She turns with a pound note in her small white hand and smiles as she watches me drown in her eyes.

"Have you a line?" I ask – (what else is there to say?).

"No. Not yet," she replies, "but it doesn't matter, I am enjoying the trip."

She moves to the back of the boat with me, and sits watching the yachts frantically fielding their spinnakers as the breeze freshens. I can't really take my eyes from her profile, answering perfunctorily the questions my passengers are putting to me. The catch that day was very small and for some reason I'm thankful.

"How lovely the light is," she murmurs.

"Is it always as rough as this?" asks a broad-faced

tattooed young man with a Midlands accent.

"This is only a slight swell," I reply. "Rough is when the prow is vertically in front of you and the ship's full of water."

"Are we going to catch anything today?"

"You should have already done so," I reply.

"You have," she says.

Yes I have, I think, more troubled than the race of water on Dancing Ledge. She looks across at the horizon and then up at the sky.

Why is she so precious to me? I've had a few girl friends ashore, but our flirtations were like the moon – as sure as they waxed, they waned. Did I catch her somehow? Or did she catch me?

And why are those eyes so strange; green one minute and aquamarine the next?

With her next to me why do I feel the rise and fall of the waves in my own stomach, and why is the beating of my own heart like the boom of the surf breaking?

"Could I have brought a rod?" someone asks.

"You could," I answered, "providing your feather trace didn't get tangled in my lines."

"Would I have caught much?" he asks.

"Depends on what's about," I reply.

"Where do you think the best place in the bay to fish is then?"

"On shore you mean?"

"Yes."

"Shep's Hollow."

"Ah yes, I know it," he says.

"Well, the sea drops there quite suddenly. If you can cast far enough you get the deep water."

"Turbot, mullet, bass?"

"Yes, any, if you're lucky."

"Mmmmmm."

An undertone from my left.

4

"I'll be there tonight."

It must have been my left; the rod and liner is looking away towards the cliffs; she is still sitting there, looking deep, deep, down into the water.

The trip over, they disembark and with the next passengers already clambering on board I cannot hope to pursue her. She walks away and watches the children netting for shrimps on the rocks. I have to draw the boat away and leave her sitting there. Shore-fishing for me tonight.

Already the moon shone like a Chinese lantern, deep and orange, low down on the horizon in a navy blue sky. Further down Ocean Bay the shore fishermen had their lines set, fishing the tide and hoping for the bass that surge shorewards in the swell. Not a hope with the sea so uncannily calm. I cast and wait. Slowly from the sea she rises clear as a moonstone; an alabaster goddess spawned by the foam. The lapping of the waves are playful echoes of kisses. The whole curtain of sea and sky is suspended motionless as she beckons and I approach. And where the wracks rock in idle motion, out of the throb of sea and tide, only the surge of foam is about my ears and I drown and drown again, in her and with her.

And when she is gone again I'm left with a singing in my ears as though listening to a thousand sea-shells.

I awoke on the same beach, my line still ridiculously propped up, catchless, in the sea. I felt the tang of salt on my mouth and there were tiny strands of seaweed in my hair.

Soon there were not enough visitors to run the trips and we brought the boats ashore. Clearing and caulking and wrapping them in tarpaulin took Ned and me most part of the autumn, leastways, the winter fires were being lit by the time we had finished.

"All ready for the next lot of satisfied customers Ned?" I said, once the job was finished.

"There's some that caught this summer more than most men have dreamed of," he said.

THE GREY LADY

O N wet days the sound of the church bells rung across the damp roofs and the pavements, and the wet stones carried the clear sound across the town and out to sea. There were days when everything was grey; the walls, the stonework, the sea, and the sky. On such days, it would be fair to say, the presence of Maggie Channon would not be noticed at all; because of all grey people she was the greyest. And she blended into the background of her surroundings like a chameleon. One was often hard put to it, to say whether she had been to an event or not; whether it was a church sale of work, an evening with slides, a wedding, or a funeral. Although it was almost certain that she had been, because she would always be asked to everything – for she was as much a part of an event as the flowers or the food.

Sometimes I would watch her in church, where she often helped in the Sunday School. I looked at her sad pale face, and glanced at her nervous white fingers, that held everything askew, as though she was unfamiliar with the true dimensions of things: simple things like gloves and hymn books and handkerchiefs. She had an expression of patient longing, mixed with gentle sadness, and she attracted sympathy as a candle flame attracts a moth. She was quiet and self-effacing and probably because she never gainsaid anything, had allowed herself to be held in the imagination of the township many years older than she actually was.

Along with my mother and aunts she was ranked as one of the stalwarts; the people who could be relied on to help in a crisis. They made tea for the fêtes, coffee for the committee meetings, and minded toddlers during the regatta. Miss Channon always gave quiet self-effacing support. She owned a small but comfortable house. She minded small relatives, nephews and nieces, and had nursed for a while a convalescent aunt; the curate's wife had stayed with her for a time, and once after a shipping accident she had put up a member of the crew of a small ship, rescued by the lifeboat. Often people finding themselves out at sea at the onset of a storm raced for the shelter of the bay and some had been blown onto the rock shelves. Once rescued they were thankful for a roof over their heads and a night's shelter.

And when it became apparent she was expecting a baby, as you can imagine, the tongues wagged apace.

The town was agog. What a time she gave the gossipping ladies of the church. Rumour and speculation were rife. It was generally agreed that old Ada Turnbull deliberately delayed dying in order to satisfy her curiosity. But she and the rest of the town were destined to be disappointed; Maggie saw to that. In her own persistent way she carried on exactly as she had always done. Perhaps she became a little less than grey, but she still managed to merge quite happily with the scenery. When the baby was born she removed herself for a week and returned with an infant daughter who was baptized Rose Marie. She was one of the town's most beautiful babies and quickly grew into one of its prettiest girls. Very slowly, following the growing up of her daughter Maggie changed. She unfolded like a rose and with the blossoming came additional colour, not so much in her and her physical appearance, but in her actions. She acquired a quiet strength. And she became one of the few people that one would not want to cross. She was never cross or angry for its own sake though; it was usually in defence of or on behalf of Rose Marie. Not that the child was spoilt; she wasn't.

Days came, days went. Tides ebbed and flowed. And the

8

years passed.

In some respects the life of the town remained unchanged. By the time Rose Marie was sixteen, though we all knew of the circumstances of her birth, she and her mother were loved and respected. And we'd grown used to the new gilded-grey Maggie.

But then I went out late one wet afternoon in winter. Already the lights were lit, and the grey-stoned front was completely deserted. Where happy, multi-coloured families had once sat roasting in the summer sun there was no one. A cold wind scattered the sand on the grey shore. I pulled out to collect some lobster pots I'd set earlier in the day. The sea was choppy and deep deep green and twinkled with the odd light from the town. But it got gloomier and more sombre as I jerked across the bay. The sun had long since disappeared over the hills and the plum colours of sunset faded swiftly, as though thankful to forego the effort of appearing cheerful. The wind freshened; I was rapidly getting colder and started to hurry. With cold hands and colder feet, and spray splashed on my face, I beached the boat after a struggle and hauled towards the sheds.

One of the doors had been opened and flapped in the breeze. I was surprised. Usually it was only Alfie or myself who had the key. But unless he'd lent it to one of the lads on the lifeboat I could have no idea who had it. Suddenly from inside the shed I heard a moan and a stifled sobbing. At first I was too frightened to do anything, and I was afraid to look into the hut.

Then out runs a woman, and dashes past me, towards the shore. She starts wading into the water, the waves breaking over the bottom of her dress making it stick to her legs. She has a scarf round her shoulders which is flying in the wind, and her long hair is wrapping itself round her face.

I followed her and she waded deeper. Now I could hear

9

above the loud splashing of the waves, her shouting, and calling and crying. It was Maggie Channon. Though whether I recognised her by sight or by instinct I shall never know. But I knew who she was. There was no moon that night and in the poor light I saw the grey, grey lady now in the deepest shades of black and slate, and I knew that all those sounds of concerted sorrow and all that human unhappiness meant that she was in a desperate mood.

I ploughed into the sea after her, struggling with the rude waves that were knocking me and jostling her. But being stronger I gained on her and having reached her pulled on her shoulder so that she should see me. Her poor eyes were blacker than the sky, and her poor broken face was the old grey of the church hall stones. The sad sad visage had crumpled and collapsed. She'd carried this image with her all her life, and I felt that all that I had ever pitied her for in the past hadn't belonged to that time at all. It had belonged to this night, to this moment. All the events of her life had been written onto her, and onto her face, she the palimpsest, and they the hieroglyphs.

I was a man now and knew that I had to hold onto her and through this crisis. Perhaps that too had been there all the time. I had sat agitatedly watching her frailty and diffidence in those church services long ago. I noticed with a shock those parts of her that were now thin and delicate like an old woman. Her shoulders were fragile, her eye sockets more shadowed and sunken and the hollows of her cheeks more gaunt.

"Maggie, Maggie!" I said. I couldn't say Miss Channon. She had been lost and lost for ever now.

"Maggie! Come on!"

Perhaps with the wind shouting so at her ears and the thud of the waves banging so, she couldn't hear.

She was shivering. But not only with cold; with fright, and shock and longing and sadness.

"Maggie. Maggie –" My voice changed. No longer curt

10

but comforting and crooning, the way my mother had comforted me.

"Maggie, there now. It's all right."

Slowly I brought her, hiccoughing and heaving, to the shore, lifting an arm about my neck and wrapping my coat about her as best I could.

She cast a backward look at the sea, way past the wild wave line, and cried out "Leave me – I'm no use – no use to her or anyone – Let me at least die –"

I took her to the shed that was open to warm her. Completely docile now, she shuddered into a deep sleep; the wind dropped and a great stillness settled over the slate-blue waves of the bay.

In less than a year's time Rose Marie would be seventeen. I went to have a word with the vicar and with the lifeboat crew – matters were wanting sorted out. From Jim the Coxswain I learnt that she had been asking questions that her mother had set her face against answering. Things were interesting me, not least the secret fire that sparkled in the blue eyes of Rose Marie. And from her I learnt that she was going away to train as a nurse, a plan she had only broken to her mother on the day I had pulled her from the sea. I learnt, too, that there were things that couldn't be spoken of between them, things that both Maggie and her daughter knew.

I went back to the vicar. It was something that I couldn't handle and he could.

None of us saw Rose Marie meet her father – a Frenchman who had been wrecked all those years ago; none of us saw his gentle greeting of Maggie who had cared for him after he'd been picked up by the lifeboat (called the *Mary Rose* in those days). Nor did we know what words they exchanged with each other, what promises had been made or broken, what hopes fulfilled or dashed. But we realised that Maggie and Rose Marie's father felt the meeting necessary or else no doubt they would not have agreed to it. How necessary it was we realised as, with the unrolling of the years, the visits recurred at the irregular intervals of a seafaring life.

That was the last we saw of the grey lady: a crystal-change spun jet and silver of her, and of her sorrow it spun content.

THE AQUARIUM

THE sign-posts did not help. You needed to know exactly where the aquarium was to be able to find it. Down the front, through a little alley, left and then a little right, and there lurking on its sleepy haunches it squatted, advertising its marvels. 'The wonders of the deep', 'The longest eel in the world', 'See the electric fish', 'Buy your souvenirs of the sea here'. Each window was painted a dull shade of blue, and each pane of glass obscured by a yellowy pea-green veil of distemper. If Miss Aggie was on the turnstile Gulley and I could either wait until she was distracted and sneak into the sub-aqueous gloom or talk away to her until she had forgotten we hadn't bought our tickets and wave us in with a sudden gesture of her little hand. Not the same with old Robinson. He'd have none of that; he'd rather not have young upstarts invade the privacy of his museum anyway. This rudeness had to be countered if honour was to be satisfied.

"Got anything more shocking than the eel then?" we'd shout.

"The plaice are in the wrong place!"

"Seen better soles on me dad's army boots!"

With a bit of effort we'd drop our own offerings into the tanks; a pink warted lobster lurked among the stones for several weeks and dying limpets lay rubbery and extended amongst the angel fish. In an inspired mood Gulley brought in a crab neatly wrapped in his sister's baby bonnet. We gave it to Miss Aggie.

"Tell your dad we've a well-dressed crab for his show," he said, and she trundled away in her wheel-chair whilst we left the exhibit and scarpered.

Poor old Robinson. Who wanted to see his soppy old

fish? Who indeed? His father had started the venture and in his time it was quite an attraction. But as the peepshows were slowly removed from the pier, the steamer made her last gasping trip to Boscombe and whelk stalls closed down, his son and Miss Aggie found the turnstiles turned ever more slowly. Miss Aggie wasn't old Robinson's real daughter anyway – it was thought she was his sister's child, born sickly and frail, abandoned by her mother who left the town after her birth. She was too sickly to go to school and most of the time she was confined to a wheel-chair. So she helped in the aquarium and added to Robinson's overheads. Small and pale, she arranged and rearranged the marine souvenirs which were laid out for inspection on a trestle table near the exit. They were labelled in her nervous handwriting: 'Shell ash tray 6d', 'Coral beads 1/6d'. She had added crochet mats, necklaces and rusty rings. Table ornaments were glued conglomorates of assorted shells; shells adorned caskets, matchbox holders, spectacle cases and pencil sharpeners. You could see the visitors eyeing them with horror and disdain.

As the fishy exhibits slowly died, or ate each other, or floated airwards with strange fungal infections, so the exhibits on sale became more profuse. Miss Aggie displayed hand-coloured postcards with views of the town, miniature globes, and purple-coloured lollipops. As trade decreased her imaginative flights of fancy increased. Strangely twisted pieces of iron were labelled: 'From a Spanish galleon wrecked after the Armada 9d', a piece of wood was 'Part of Robinson Crusoe's raft 10½d', a yellowy-scratched piece of ivory announced it had been 'Part of Captain Ahab's leg 1/4d'. Mermaids' combs cost 7d and mermaids' purses 4d. Gulley and I heard the snorts of laughter and the cries of incredulity – for days now the turnstiles would not move at all.

The season was gathering to its final few weeks, the trades-people announced bargains, slashed prices, offered

14

services half price. The last scramble for the pennies that would see us through the winter was on. No one believed when she arrived that the stout blonde lady, with seamed stockings and red nail polish was old Robinson's sister – yet it seemed she was – and her loud voice sent plangent echoes into the submarine depths of the aquarium.

The notice went up overnight, 'Real live mermaid, Entrance 2/-' Two shillings! Would people really pay 2/-to see a mermaid? Oh we would! Gulley and I racked our brains, searched our pockets, bullied our relatives; all to get the precious couple of bob. Once or twice we went to see if Miss Aggie was on the door – when we might stand a chance. But she never was. It was always Robinson's sister – boasting of their sea prize – advertising its beauty – emphasising the rare opportunity presented to the public.

Then the notice said '2 more days only' – we eavesdropped on the outcoming crowds – but they seemed silent and numb.

One more day – 'Last day to see the mermaid' roared the sign. We had sixpence ha'penny between us. We were desperate. The day passed. Then Gulley found it – a florin – sun-winking silver on the sand!

"You go," I said, "and tell me all about it."

" 'Snot fair – we only want another one and five pence ha'penny. Perhaps I could put it on a horse."

I think he'd learnt the expression from his father. "Yer don't know how," I called his bluff.

"No, yer right," he conceded.

"But they say money makes money," he said plaintively.

We gazed at the piece, hoping it might divide gently in half like an amoeba. It didn't.

"We'll wait," said Gulley and added – "we'll wait till the very end of the day and then we'll see if she'll let us both in for half a crown."

"She'd never!"

"She might. I believe everyone who wants to see it will have seen it by then. It's worth a try. She can only say no."

Never had the sun moved its shadows so slowly from the eastern cliff to the rocky foreland. We presented ourselves down the back alleys at five to five precisely. There was no one there.

Robinson's sister picked at a fingernail. Gulley was inspired.

"Are we too late?" he switched on wide-eyed eagerness.

"What for?"

"The mermaid –"

"You'd have to hurry – I'm about to close up."

"Oh I will – I say – will you let me and my friend in for half a crown? – seeing as we won't stay long."

She looked at us: "Go in then – but I'm closing this door now – so you'd better get your skates on."

We dashed in.

"Hmm, I'd like to see 'er with skates on – big 'uns, all flattened over 'er 'ead," Gulley said quietly as we groped through the soupy vertiginous atmosphere. As we scurried past the illuminated rectangles of swimming green he carried on under his breath: "Barging in the way she did. I've not seen poor old Aggie once since she came – hey, did yer mum come?"

"What, 'ere?"

"Yeah."

"To see the mermaid?"

"Mm."

"No. She said she didn't hold with staring at freaks."

"Oh," Gulley gulped.

"Oh," I sighed.

In front of us a sign displayed the attraction. The water, if it was possible, was even more murky and oleaginous.

Green algae seemed to have swept a curtain over the glass. We peered in. Noses pressed and squashed. There were rocks, there was a lot of weed, a lot of weed and crouched near the back in a miniature cave, dully lit by a painted light bulb, a shrivelled despondent figure, seeming to field her mane of swimming hair. Despite all the water she seemed dehydrated and the light gave her flesh the sheen of malachite, sickly and dying. I shuddered.

Then a voice stridently bounced round the corners of stone.

"Everyone out. That's it: show's over."

The bulk approached.

"Come on you two, 'op it!"

We turned to go – but not until we'd seen the mermaid's tresses part and the anxious eyes of Miss Aggie peer dully through the waving fronds of seaweed.

Gulley and I scarpered.

All through the winter the work went on. Scaffolding came and went. Paint pots, ladders, saws, and planks were parked against the wall. The little lost alley had never had so much traffic. Then a glaring sign announced 'Fish and Chip Parlour' and the aquarium disappeared forever.

It was my mum who said that I'd be happy to take Miss Aggie out. She'd been in the cottage hospital all winter but needed fresh air now the balmier weather of spring was softening the winter breezes and the spring sun was coaxing warmth and life from the earth.

So Gulley and I pushed her chair carefully over the uneven paving stones and round over the swollen stream up towards the church and the duck pond. The willows had veiled themselves like brides in green, a miasmic haze of yellow-young growth.

There was already a small group of children throwing crusts to the ducks, who launched themselves onto the millpond with the insouciance of the well-sated. It was when Gulley was chasing a lazy drake that the accident happened. Suddenly Miss Aggie was sprawled on the ground, but by the time he returned I had gathered her up and was quickly putting her blankets back round her and tucking her little legs back under their covers.

"Not to worry dears," she said. "I'm all right, really I am," and the children carried on pelting the ducks with bread. I insisted on getting Miss Aggie home as quickly as I could, trying not to look as white and glazed as I felt.

Spring took a further hold on the land, crocuses spread out gold petals to the sun and the sky repainted itself several shades deeper of cerulean blue; the sea not to be outdone washed over its slate shades with aquamarine.

The day I took Miss Agggie to the little beach the other side of the quay had little puffballs of cloud racing merrily from the shore to the seaward sky. Our silent walks had corroborated our conspiracy – I couldn't even tell Gulley of the glimpse I had got of those wizened scale-covered legs, that tapered into a single limb. . .

"Let's have an ice shall we?" she asked, gazing out at the sea where I'd left her chair; "my treat, to thank you for all the times you've taken me on our little excursions."

I said I'd go and see if the kiosk was open, yet. When I returned the chair was empty, the rugs thrown to one side. There was only the slightest gentle groove running in the sand from the chair to the sea. They never found a body and my mum said they decided it was an open verdict. I told no one how I'd seen a head, which turned momentarily from the deep water, back to where I was standing alone on the beach, two ice cream cones in my hand. How a hand had raised itself out of the waves. But was it waving or drowning?

DAVY JONES' LOCKER

I never once thought of breathing. It all seemed so natural, sliding beneath the surface, watching the sun sparkle through the heaving roof of the sea, and seeing it paddling and dappling the sand on the sea bed.

Past the beds of waving wrack and past the green slime-covered rocks I drifted. All was in gentle motion, from the rocking waves to the weeds floating idly in the water, forwards and backwards like long tresses of hair. Green glass water all around, and the singing of sucking currents in my ears; I felt deep and plump with contentment. The hypnotic, ever-swinging of the seaweeds was like a lullaby. Deeper umber shadows reached out from the rocks, thick velvet hangings breathing and pulsating with the rhythm of the waves. The sibilance increased as though a long sweet harmonic note had been struck and held very softly. I thought idly of the sirens' song as I floated through this strange harmonic kingdom; but not intentionless. All the time I knew I was wanted somewhere; pace might not be important, but eventual arriving was. Two large silver-speckled fish flashed past, weaving their way unerringly through the rocks and fronds. There were more rocks underneath me now. And still the same tugging urgency.

I saw limpets lifting and stretching themselves from their rocks and barnacles extending their frail ferny ends into the water; mussels and cockles gulped as I passed and gently yawned wider as I washed over them. The singing and humming, like a thousand sea-shells calling from coral strands, grew louder, the crescendo, like a current of motion, sweeping me deeper and darker to murky fathoms below. All this dark world throbbed with the echo of the sea-song, richer and deeper now with the basses adding a thrumming pulse to the sound. A sense of nearly having arrived pervaded me.

Here the sea was colder; strange overdressed fish ogled me, whilst shoals of tiny green and yellow fish darted out of their way.

They lumbered around in their semi-blind world like brightly lit double decker buses, blundering through the gloom of a pea-souper. Strange anaemic ribbons of sea weed strained vainly for the surface, dead brains of convoluted coral crouched under iron-bound boulders.

Gently the cold seduced my limbs. The darkness encompassed all my periphery. Now through the indigo shadows I could see dead men's hands lifting and dropping with the rhythm of the tides; pale lights glowed on either side of me, floating in tantalising formations like will o' the wisps. I seemed to follow them, or they seemed to lead me and the whole seemed to be them singing and their coldness scorching me.

The lights increased; the glare spread in a circle around me like a trail of gunpowder being lit and I saw, or thought I saw strange images, some near, some far. I couldn't focus properly on them, and in bringing them into the scope of my vision I destroyed them: sea elephants clapping and waving their flippers, conducting a wild sea-symphony; bony fingers throwing open and rifling chests full of gold pieces; wild women whose green tresses swept over their soft purple eyes and whose waists tapered into thick fleshy fish-tails; octopuses wrapped sinuously round each other like entwined shivas, and an army of sea anemones, their tentacles fluttering in an orange and red jetstream, pouring past me.

Suddenly there was a crash of waves and the sea seemed to part, but what were waves were the manes of white horses, and great steeds brushed me over into the sand. I lay there, all the breath gone from me, and watched the dolphins thunder by and arching and falling green-bodied tritons, with dark-blue nipples, swelling the din by calling on their conches. Shrieking and laughing children on sea-horses and crabs blowing bubbles at each other careered past; then the flash of gold tridents, enormous bunches of thick white hair, and eyes that looked forwards and backwards through the wave-tunnel of time. I felt stricken with a thunderbolt of coldness and the wild singing and surging seemed to break all around my ears as Calypso followed in the wake of the band. Scarcely had the feeling of awe given way to despair and a sense of rejection when the all-swamping vortex of her arrival tore me and thundered through me.

The deep aquatic harmony of the sea had broken into a screaming roar; the dissonant scratching of the surf snarling at the land, the waves tearing viciously at the sand, the spume raking the pebbles backwards and forwards with clutching fingers. I was being thrown back and out. . .and away. . .

The cold retreated. I saw penguins shooting under the soft moulded ceiling of an ice-floe; the blanched face of the second engineer of the *Mary Rose* under his peaked cap; the sudden shimmer of mother-of-pearl against the ceiling of flesh-soft pink, the closed and secret parts of a nautilus shell. Clambering round and round into a spiralling interior I twisted and turned whilst shouting and roaring throbbed and hurt my ear drums; round me the ever-reddening roof and nacre floor pressed tighter and tighter. The tunnel became darker and darker and the struggle for light and air began. Pushing and straining, gasping and spluttering, choking and bursting, all gathered to a peak and broke.

I opened my eyes.

When they told me later I'd been in the sea for half an hour, and disappeared from sight for ten minutes I didn't believe them. When later I told the doctor what I'd seen and how it all ended he said simply 'birth trauma' and I didn't believe him either. How come only I knew that Alfie Jones the second engineer had broken his front tooth when he was thrown from the ship, so that later when his body was washed ashore I was the only person to recognise that gappy mouth?

LIMPET LIL

I'VE called her wild names; the old woman who gathers the agates. Wild names that match her wild eyes. But every day she goes, down on the wind-swept shore, along by the banks of gravel, looking for her milky white stones. She knows, from all of the pebbles, at a glance, which are her children. And grabs them to her, like a child that's strayed, with a quiet quick reprimand. Her bright eye glances over the shells, and the shelves upon shelves of stones. Suddenly she rises very quickly to claim what she could only have glimpsed from the corner of her eye.

I never knew the names she gave them, but to her they were all the fruits of the sea. She spun and washed, and ground and polished them, until they gleamed like sunshine. Oranges and ochres, purples and lakes, gamboge and crimson, sienna and terra cotta. Princes of Tyre in their purple held goblets encrusted with these, and the tin merchants of famed Phoenicia traded ivory for just such. Although sea-fashioned jewels had been fashioned from many, most had been given back to the sea.

Galleys and galleons lay laden, grinning at the mirror of calm, knowing their secret treasures that they had laid back on the breast of the sea. We own nothing and can take nothing with us, the shipwrecked sailors cried; return us to Amphitrite sobbed the drowning, we own nothing and take nothing away.

Although we knew where she lived, we never ventured there. Her old pitch shed stood hidden, half-hidden in the clefts of the cliffs. The wood was like the dark brown slimy palings that propped up the decaying pier; the forest of tarry and bladder-wrack strewn timbers that formed the half world of its underside. We plagued and taunted her with catcalls and whistles and by tossing the old slipper limpets at her one old window. It stared like a tired eye, with paralysed lid and rheumy sill out across the boulders of old cliff falls. She paid us no attention; she continued her dancing walk along the beach, appearing to curtsey and genuflect like a giddy nun, or drunken weathercock.

"It'll all go back," she said, "just you see."

On the cold nights of winter she'd be fashioning the filigree – and preparing her children for their hosts. Decking them in the finest regalia, suiting each jewel to its fitting.

When the first spring visitors bowled over the hills into the town, she'd be out in her best hat with the nodding marguerite, setting her little stall on the front.

Kiosks and shops removed the boards from their fronts; the hatches which had been battened down against the winter gales, all were now carefully removed.

With the care of a gardener she set colour against colour and metal against metal. She stood and admired the effect. As the first buyers approached her eyes clouded green and grey, and the wildness of thrown spray darted across them. After the purchase she whispered "Bye, bye, my babies, you'll come back to me." And the smug waxiness of the agates knowing the truth glowed with a deep inward light, the brown rich marbles chuckled in their chestnut throats.

So they took all and left her nothing – as she took all that she found, leaving the beach bare – and they gave it all back as she knew they must. And all that was left was desolation. And the great wide loneliness of the sea. For it was that great call of solitude that was the look in her eyes. It is that call of the gulls. It is that which grips the stomach, thrills and appals the imagination. The wide gold mudflats at sunset, the little chill on the breeze and the rills in the sand – the tiny etched wrinkles on the top of the water and the little tired waves that hardly spill onto the sand. It's all

24

the echo of alone. Of alone and of a time before, when nothing breathed or rose or swelled on land – when there was only sea.

PUNCH AND JUDY MAN

WOULD that I saw what they saw, gaudy stripes, barley twists, and sugar-candy colours. An oriental box of delights surmounted by rococo curlicues in the finest fairground scrolls and whirls. And once the velvet swooped aside, the slapstick and hilarity. Heaven forbid they should see what I see. But I stay out of sight. Behind me the sea, swinging backward and forward across the sands so that some days I'm forward and some days I'm backward. The sibilance somehow softens the silence. And those dismembered limbs of mine weave through a dance of their own, way above my head. They know the forms, the signs, the signals without me. They cajole and entice laughter and fear and shrieks from their audience. The white, blond, dark, little heads swivel and strain, toss and lurch. The're shrieks, howls and warning cries – "Behind yer," "Behind yer," "Behind yer." They build to a crescendo and the sound breaks like a wave. And skittle and skattle go the hands and the sound echoes round and round my black hot perspiring prison.

So the sea softens me. I feel its quiet waters nuzzling my broken punch-drunk puppet figure. It was like that once. When I left the nick, not a farthing to my name. My mother dead, Auntie Emmie gone. My mates had fled and the rest of the family – well, they didn't want to know. I'd met Mac inside and he taught me a few tricks, playing the spoons, tearing newspaper, and re-arranging cards so quick the eye couldn't see. So I spent a few years doing the theatre queues – those times when the little camp stools followed the gutters round, from the flashy front entrance to the seedy stage door. And mostly I was all right and didn't often sleep out – not unless I had to.

And then I met Eth. She was good in her way and honest and hardworking. She'd done a bit of leg-kicking, and I became the Great Orsino.

The hands scamper and a howl goes up. One of the kids has dropped his ice cream. I can see it there on the ground, white and gritty in the sand. People still pass, trying not to pay attention, pretending they've seen it all before, trying hard not to become engrossed. Those wizard's wands of mine know and they make hypnotic passes and induce hypnotic trances. The steps slow and stop, the feet falter and the eyes focus slowly as the tension oozes gently from tight shoulders onto the pavement. The consoling sea behind sings and surges, and the voices carouse away; the measure continues, the story unwinds and the tale will have to run its course.

So we saved, Eth and I, enough to retire to the sea; John joined the Navy and Bridey went to live in Harlow New Town. She was tough on me, Eth; she fairly bamboozled me, when I wanted a quiet time or a bit of a drink or a night out with the lads. She always was a bossy girl. When she was head girl once in the chorus the girls all called her The Boss. And it was take off your shoes and wipe your feet and hang up yer coat and put out the cat. And rock the baby and peel the spuds.

With a thwack say the hands and a thwack they say. And bang with the stick. Take that. Take that. And they throw the baby out the window and bang the wife on the head.

Hoh! goes the breath as the audience expires and the waves suck back the sloping shingle.

Hoh! so I fell, so beaten, so battered, so ready to lie down and die.

Sometimes I'd look at her and wonder what she was thinking. I'd wonder when I looked at her red knuckles how she managed. When I caught her on all fours with her hands in the bucket, wringing the old cloth and cleaning the floors. Or when she hurried in from shopping with her clothes all dampish and a cold drip of moisture hanging from her nose. You drive yourself, Eth. You work too hard. But she'd smile and say "Come on Alf it's all worth it – we'll retire to the sea, just you see – one day".

The Great Orsino went on tour and played variety in the halls and the kids got bigger; we had our fights and our brawls. I saw her once give Bridey a hiding and I lay into her because I'd been on the beer. She gave me a back hander quick and heavy and I never laid a finger on her again. Oh, the slap of the sea and the sob of the pebbles.

So they chase each other round the stage, they do, faster and faster, panting and furious. Thwick. Thwack. Bang and crash!

Hurray! They all call, hurray, hurray.

But I'm beaten and broken in here in my prison. The hand's agitation seems to avoid my heart. I can't get worried, or care, or affected. The waves I think seem to soothe me to sleep.

So we came here at last, on a day trip to begin with. Eth stood and stood and gazed at the sea. We were lucky. We had walked from the place the coach dropped us, up a short gentle rise which led to the beach. In front was a shelter, crowned with a clock, decorated in blue and cream and white. And the road fell away and the sea was ahead, deep and again deep; deepest blue and the smell on the air was the smell of seaweed. We stood and we watched and we slowly started walking, gently together, towards the cluster of the town.

"We must stay here," said Eth and I nodded. I agreed. Her plan, our plan, for the future was completely agreed.

I toured a bit more and topped a few bills. Old Johnny Stevens who was a third of The Tuneful Triplets had lent me a swazzle and we'd made a few puppets and when television started emptying the end of pier palaces we did the odd kid's birthday or the occasional party.

But I was getting on and Eth was becoming ill. Then our John was busted for having some dope. I've no respect for the law. They've only ever messed me up – I have no fondness for the boys in blue.

The gulls seem to shriek in panic not laughter as the hands follow each other and hit the old bobby down.

But we got him off we did, which was a relief and a let out, and it meant Eth and I could get away at last. So we came here, to this place, this gem on the coast, and we bought a small house and hung curtains at the windows. But Eth was not well and they took her to a home. And there she malingered for a year or two. Dying, slowly, piece by piece, negligently dropping her bodily functions. The doctors were no good. They ought to try their own medicine and pay for it too.

Thwack the hands say, thwack and again thwack – thwack the quack and someone calls out that's the best way to do it.

To meet the extra bills I needed more work, although I'd decided to myself I'd retired. But there was nothing for it – but to go back on the boards – well, to send the hands back even if the heart didn't follow.

So I sit here each day; bemused, amazed; at the chases, and the shenanigans and the fiasco up above. I wonder who can involve themselves so earnestly in such a fiction.

And the kids scream for more, and laugh, and cry, and the sand is covered with their brown jolly bodies.

But the waves call for peace, beat up and beat down, and each day I put the booth where I can hear their kind sound.

IN A BLINK OF TIME'S EYELIDS

I N the tight-throated early morning we had walked past the giddy cliffs and followed the primrose track over the eerie caves. Now, clambering down the cliff face, we peered in at the entrance of several of them, shouting madly to hear the echo thrown back at us, with overtones of seaweed and waves. The muffled tones of the sea glanced off the shiny walls and fell silent at last on the bed of dead shingle at our feet. At last we found the one we were making for, already knee high in water; the tide had swollen into this crevice as it did daily. So we waded into it. Behind us the brightness of daylight, before us the gloom of the cave. Two different worlds, and us like spirits of the newly departed wandering between them.

There was, however, nothing vague in our path; determined wades through the water took us to the back of the cavern. There, pulled high up on a shore of black shingle, lay the boat. Our boat, which we had spent so many days working on. We had mended her and her old hull and seams, we had set right the rowlocks and eventually begged a pair of oars off my uncle. I think he knew by now what was going on and why Tim and I had been so quiet and inconspicious this long summer holiday. We were like children with a new toy. Well, we were children with a new toy. We bubbled with excitement. Gently ragging and vaguely ribbing each other, our conversation was only an undercurrent murmur of delight that had to use the form of words because we'd been taught that way. And we had to use argumentative forms because that assured a rhythmic two-way communication. Parry and reposte; a wave breaking and then receding.

"Mind me arm!"

"You nudged me!"

"I'm trying to hurry."

"You can't hurry wading through water."

"I know, its pushing back. Blast! There's some slopped over the top of me boots."

"Pass me the bag."

"You can't manage it as well."

"Oh yes I can! I'm stronger than you."

"Oh yes, stronger. Who needs the help stirring the tar?"

"Oh I never. It was while it was cold."

"Oh it could't be. . ."

"Oh, I say, look out!"

"Sorry; hey! Where's the bag now?"

"Here; oh there she is. Isn't she as magnificent as we thought?"

"Alley-opp!"

"Oooops – Oh gosh!"

"Look out!"

"Mind me head! I'm not a dwarf."

"Only look like one. No. Put the oar. . ."

"Yes, I know. . ."

"I only said – like that; and. . ."

"Can I row first?"

"Why should you?"

"Why not?"

"Why not? Okay. Go on then, I'll push you off. . ."

"Wait then. . . oh, I said wait. . ."

"Too late. Row!!!"

"Row? I've not even got the oars – well, you steer then."

"Me? Me steer! What are you supposed to be doing with the oars?"

Scraping, clattering, the sound of wood echoing strangely and the sharp noise of the pebbles against the keel; manipulation out of the narrow cave entrance, then with an increasing draught of water under the boat we made the arch of the cave, the cliffs swung away from us like a receding backdrop and we were on the high seas.

I can't honestly remember which of us it was who first got the idea of a wreck chart. But together, spurred on by the rough diagram in the lifeboat station, we collected as many naval charts as we could between us. Then came the idea of compiling our own information and of course, having verified the existence of a wreck and marked its position on our map, then we had to confirm our findings and explore it. We were thorough in our research and the additional excitement was that no one else knew anything about it. Hence the work on *Lady Jayne*. For having found her by no more than a happy accident it was as though the sea itself was giving us the freedom to authenticate some of our claims. We even knew the names of some of the ships down there – the *Endymion*, the *Lorna Grey* and the *Archimedes*; but the biggest and best was the Spanish galleon *San Salvador*.

High above us the fulmars and guillemots wheeled and circled, some tiny specks lost against the floss of the creamy clouds. The tide pitched between ebb and flow was ideal. Using the lighthouse and a couple of rocks to take bearings, we estimated after rowing for about an hour that we had arrived in the right position. Using a make-shift dead weight as an anchor we could begin our search for the wreck.

Tim was a stronger swimmer than I, and in fact a better diver because he was more powerful; but I could stay down longer because I could hold my breath.

One of us was always in the boat, with a life-line; after all, the last thing we wanted was to be hauled over the coals by angry adults because we had been stupid over safety precautions – and because we were on our own we were determined to do everything according to the book.

Diving commenced.

Tim was on first shift. I admit I became more interested in the fillings in the sandwiches. I wondered what adults found so fascinating in fish paste that they didn't in mixtures like peanut butter and banana. When I grew up and made my own sandwiches I decided I'd mix whatever two things came to hand. That way I'd be sure of really interesting sandwiches, that didn't seem all bread.

Tim clambered aboard.

"Your turn Tubby."

"Why Tubby?"

"All that food you've been eating."

"No I've not. I've had one sandwich."

"I bet."

"Well, I have. I was thinking about them more than eating them."

"Oh yes. I can just see you. . . thinking about food and not eating it."

"Well, anyway, I wouldn't be stuffing myself if I was about to dive."

"Oh yes you would. . . You'd dive with a six course dinner inside you and sink like a stone."

"It's not the weight that makes it dangerous, so there!"

"I know, stupid."

"I'm not stupid."

"Well go and do some diving then."

"Did you find anything?"

"No, not a sausage."

"Nothing at all?"

"Should we move out a bit?" I suggested.

"Well I reckon I swam in a fifty yard quadrant between here and those rocks there so you'd better cover the next bit round."

"What. There to about there. . .?"

"Mmmm. Yes."

"Well – we could move out a bit," he conceded.

"Hang on then, I'll haul up the anchor."

"Let me get a jersey on, the wind's freshening."

"Yes, you're right."

"Still it's safe enough for a while" (referring to the weather). "If it looks at all bad, I'll bring you up."

"Okay."

We moved off shore a bit and then over the side I went. There's no really idyllic underwater world when you're diving without special Scuba equipment. The banging of your heart, the straining of the face muscles and the creaking sensation you get in your chest, all tend to become major obsessions. What one sees around one is merely peripheral. But you pick up a lot quickly. You rapidly notice, note and appraise, casting aside what is not important very quickly. The eye alights and judges in a split second. It is all scanning, pursuing and a quick belt to the surface to refuel with oxygen.

Almost at once I noticed that what I was swimming over was not just stones covered with seaweed. Up and gulp. Then down again, more look, hold and feel; probe with fingers, looking, feeling, for something to tear off with the fingers, to bring back to the surface to examine with more air in the lungs. But there's nothing. All so slippery and slimy because of the years and years its been lying in the sea. Up, up up again. Shouting to Tim and him giving me a quick thumbs up sign but indicting a heavy rain-saturated cloud glowering on the horizon.

"One more," I shout.

"Okay, But that's your lot."

Back to the green world of waving fronds and algae encrusted. . . what? – Spars? Masts? Cannons? I couldn't tell. But it wasn't just rocks. Something more like metal hit my fingers. I looked, clung, wrenched, struggled, but whatever it was was not going to yield. Two messages shouted for ascendance in my head – one to resurface, the other to find some clue as to what I had discovered. Self-survival won, and my life-line was given a couple of tugs as well. I was swauled, a mixture of swimming and being hauled, to *Lady Jayne*.

"Quick, quick. We must get more sheltered."

"Heavens," I muttered.

Already the rain was spattering the surface of the water, breaking and pitting the tops of the sea so that it looked like a sponge.

"Help me pull," said Tim. "Take an oar."

I did, and we needed it. For twenty minutes we pulled to the shore. Two things were with us. The wind was on shore and the tide was flowing. . . otherwise in that swell *Lady Jayne* would have been feeling at a severe disadvantage. We made the cave after another hour and pulled her high up on the shore. Then we moved her higher, and higher, and then there wasn't a shore at all and we were perched on a ledge with the painter tied round our ankles. We ate the rest of the sandwiches and discussed my find.

"It could be anything," said Tim.

I was inclined to agree with him.

"I'm sorry," I said miserably, "there just wasn't enough time to get anything that might help."

"Well, we'll still find out. – Why is your mother so obsessed with fish paste? You'd think she of all people would be fed up to the back teeth with fish."

"I don't know."

"That rain suddenly arrived from nowhere."

"Sure did."

"Won't last. Too much fair weather cloud around earlier."

Tides turn eventually and even the strongest squalls blow themselves out. Because we'd rested and eaten we felt we couldn't possibly miss another possible afternoon. The tide was on the way out, which meant at least the shore would be nearer and provided the wind didn't change or blow violently we'd be moderately safe. True, once the boat was out in the open again, the rain had passed and the brief squall ended as suddenly as it had begun.

Back at the same spot as well as we could judge, once again. Tim decided he should go first and sure enough on the first dive he found it.

"Oh boy! You're right," he breathed heavily. "There is definitely something there. I'm going down again."

His wet head vanished as he up ended, and down went his feet.

What awoke me? What triggered off an alarm in my head? Was it the sudden harsh shriek of a seagull? or the screech of too much silence?

Suddenly I decided to pull the life line and to pull it hard. There was a dead weight on the end, so I pulled and pulled until Tim's body floated up to the surface. Panic-stricken, I knew I'd never get him into the boat. So I jumped over the side and pulled his head and chin up under my crooked arm, stretching out with my free arm to the boat. Involuntarily I jerked my knee up under his shoulders and the blow made him choke. Choke and breathe. I heard him gasp.

Still holding him, I shouted "Tim. Tim. Are you all right?"

"Ooo-er" and there was lots of deep breathing.

"Can you get into the boat?"

"Mm, think so."

How did we manage it? I don't know. But we did. He collapsed on the bottom of the boat, coughing and vomiting. And then just lying still. I covered him with all the clothes I could find and then the first flash of lightning hit the water, somewhere near the eastern horizon. The sky had turned violet like a bruise and the nervous breeze that scampers about the wave tops before a storm shivered past me. I sat down to row to the shore, not out of reach providing the wind didn't swing. But I knew sudden gusts can be unpredictable and in a storm they can run in any direction. Double basses ran up and down two octaves – the thunder had arrived. The waves lost their tops and started breaking rank, scattering spume and foam. The rhythm of rowing was very easily broken. First the lightning, then the thunder; sometimes grumbling away beneath the horizon, sometimes cracking overhead with an abruptness that made me jump. The rain and the sea seemed to melt together, such was the fury with which the sky met the ocean. I was tired and aching with all the swimming and pulling and rowing and the boat seemed to get heavier and heavier.

Soon one event ran into another, and what seemed hours of effort merged into one long horrifying minute. Waves started breaking into the little boat and we had too much water aboard. When the shore still seemed no nearer I lost an oar. I could hear the plunging and rushing of water all round me; the dark clouds, shredded and torn, fled across the horizon; the shore, the land, safety, were my only goals. Then the other oar went. I only hoped we were near enough to the shore to be swept there by the waves alone. Then just when it seemed we were being rushed forward in the right direction, an enormous wave reared high behind us and broke over the stern. I grabbed Tim by the throat and fell down into the cold, cold, icy, mad turbulence. There were shouts and screams all around me, all echoing backwards and forwards in time, as though I was in the vortex of some enormous whirlpool. And then there were other voices, and lights, and Uncle's kind face.

"There lad, there you're all right."

"All right now."

"Steady. Steady on there."

"Where's Tim?"

"He's all right. You'll both be all right."

"Stand back there. Let the ambulance through."

"Ambulance? Who needs an ambulance Uncle?"

"You do!"

"Not Tim?"

"Both of you. Just checking."

"Aah"

"Silly children. What were you doing?"

All dissembling stopped.

"Looking for wrecks."

"Well you've certainly added another."

"Oh – *Lady Jayne*?"

"She'll be all right, I expect, when she's baled out. Hush now. Rest."

We weren't kept long in the hospital. A few days later Tim's parents and my Uncle brought our clean clothes in for us so we could leave in the morning.

Sitting in the sunshine, waiting to be picked up, a spruce and portly nurse came up to us.

"Something for you."

"What, me?" said Tim.

"Yes lad, you're forgetting something."

"What on earth?" said Tim.

"Your bathing trunks; your parents didn't take them with them and they were left in your locker."

"Oh Lord yes," said Tim. "Thanks a lot, Nurse."

We had been separated in the hospital.

"Did your parents get mad at you, Tim?"

"Oh no, not really. They were more worried about you. And your Uncle."

"Oh, he's okay."

"Evidently there've been dreadful freak storms since we've been resting here. I'd heard the rain, but didn't know it was that bad."

"Yes, that's what my uncle said."

"Am I glad he was on that shore and spotted us so soon."

"Yes, would you believe it, he'd come with some extra rations – he knew all the time where *Lady Jayne* was, and checked her himself."

"Cheek."

"That's probably why he let us have the oars."

"True."

"But even he was surpirsed with the speed at which the storm broke, so they can't be mad at us."

"You going to tell your mum?"

"What, and spoil her yearly visit to my aunty? No I can't. If Uncle had thought it serious he would have called her back himself."

"I expect it was her fish paste that gave you so much fortitude."

"Doubtless; I shall never say another word against it."

"That's good then."

"Why?"

"There's something I'm going to show you. . . but I want you to promise you won't say anything about it to anyone."

"Okay," I said, alerted by his tone, "what is it?"

Trembling slightly, and agitated, he started fingering desperately in the pocket of his trunks. And then produced it. Exquisitely worked in gold – gleaming redly in the morning sun – and saying proudly round the rim 'San Salvadore'.

"Why say nothing though?"

"In case others go there, and find it. Our wreck. Our galleon. And tear it apart using their expensive underwater equipment and oxyacetylene. Anyway this is half yours. But I don't want anyone to know. Do you understand?"

"Of course I do," I said. "But you keep it, Tim; after all you nearly died for it."

"Would have done, if it hadn't been for you."

"Perhaps would not have done if I'd been a bit quicker."

"Oh, I don't know, my dad says you can drown in a trice, and anyway you rowed me all the way back to the shore."

"It wasn't far."

"Oh only in a force nine gale. Of course not. A doddle. Just like a duck pond, a cruise down the Thames."

The idea was to keep the medallion six months each. Later, much later we'd show it to the British Museum. Sometimes nowadays I show it to the grandchildren and tell them the exciting story of how we found it.

But we need not have been so secretive. Uncle had spent quite a time trying to authenticate the wreck. He knew enough about the sea to be able to have a fair idea of whereabouts we were when the storm broke, especially as he had been so near to the shore, and knew where *Lady Jayne*'s secret mooring place was. Later he told me that in fact the whole area had been searched by a team of divers, but nothing had been found at all.

Perhaps the storm had dislodged what was there, broken it up or thrown it all even further out to sea. Or buried it for ever, for at the same time parts of the cliffs had fallen, we were told. And I always wondered why it was the treasure had been pure gold, showing no signs of having been nearly five hundred years in the sea. Had the earlier squall uncovered some hoarding place which the storm later destroyed entirely? In which case, how strange that between these two times was when Tim dived down there. Like a door opening and closing once in five hundred years, and he being the one allowed to peep through and take away a tiny piece of that age. Whether what we managed to salvage at considerable risk in that brief blink of the eyelids of time was worth it, I don't know. Well, yes I do. Scrupulously every six months we give it back again.

THE DREAM

I lay on the cropped green grass above the cliffs; the sea-thrift, the clover, and the harebells were all the same colour as the chalk hill and adonis blue butterflies. The air was loud with the humming of insects and, below, the deep sound of the waves forever collapsing with laughter in the lap of the rock at the foot of the cliffs. I was nearly asleep. Half of me dozed while the other half roamed on the magic wings of fancy – completely unfettered by the deep relaxation of my limbs and body. The wind was gentle and soft and the air smelt of salt and honey. The warm sun made honey of everything beneath it. I slept. I dozed. I hovered between sleeping and waking like a somnambulist. I hovered between dream and reality, like a cloud near the horizon. I was neither sea nor sky but something in that purple smudge between the two.

A girl stood between me and the sun.

She was panting slightly, her arms akimbo. Her legs brown and bruised and her hair white. I imagined she'd clambered up the cliff. A pretty reckless undertaking, but not impossible.

"My sister's down there," she gasped. "Trapped down on the beastly beach. Will it be covered at high tide?"

I stopped to think: time of year, time of day – "Probably not," I granted. I didn't like being jerked awake like that. I didn't like being interrupted. Anyway why and how did they get there – and how trapped?

"She caught her foot, I think," replied the other.

"What do you mean, you think?"

"I think she did, she didn't really say. She just said go and get help – I think the tide may come right up here."

41

I looked at her. I wondered if she was barmy.

"Did you try and help?" I said.

"I did; she said it didn't work."

"Why not?", I replied.

"I thought she was stuck. She is – she will die."

"Why. . . I mean, what do you think I can do?" I asked.

"I don't know," she said. "Get help I suppose; yes. . . yes. . . get help, or come back down with me."

"Did you actually see her foot trapped or not?" I was getting cross and petulant. I had difficulty believing this was real. I wasn't made for cliff rescues. Dramatic savings of life weren't my line of business. Anyway the time was wrong. It was a lazy day; a day of inaction – and this girl didn't belong to reality nor did her story. It was all far too sensational and over dramatic. She had probably made it up or dreamt it. Or more likely, I had made it up – made her up and dreamt her – and dreamt the whole story that placed me so clearly and cleverly in the role of the hero, with a heroine so close at hand. She calls the coastguard while I climb down the cliff – I free her sister and land her halfway to safety, we are forced to sit tight when she finds she cannot make the next bit up the cliff, and finally we are plucked like flies off a wall by the Cliff Rescue Service, while the lifeboat stands by and a winsome chopper beats the waves backwards, anxiously watching our every move. No. . . No. . . this is my romantic nature – this girl the conjuring of my imagination – my Guinevere, my Isolde, my fair maid of Astelot. All this flooded my head like a cloudburst of cold and spiky rain. I groaned, I think a little, and rolled over. . .

The springy grass scratched my legs, the heavy lightish air swamped me. The hum and scurry of happy insects swarmed about me and the nectar-thick smell of the flowers intoxicated me. I blinked and turned again to face her.

"Well, if you really think. . ." I began, tugging at a clover flower.

But she had gone; the light seemed brighter where she had stood and the air was shimmering now in the glorious heat.

I sat up. And my eyes scanned further afield. I span through a circle – and then stood to see if she had run down over the brow of the undulations in the ground. But not a sign was there of her – not a sound, only still the buzzing flies and slapping waves.

Far, far away the horizon danced in inscrutable amethyst; in the bay the toy boats bobbed about with a smug jauntiness. Each cheeky wavelet captured the eye of the silver sun, once mirrored its light and winked at me – one flash and then passed on.

When I read later in the newspapers of two sisters being caught by the rising tide – one with her foot trapped by a heavy rock and the other apparently trying to help her – I couldn't help feeling I had dreamt everything that had happened before, subsequently. One of those weird occasions where time seems cheated, and what happened after the event, for a long time appears to have happened before. But ever and again I am obsessed by those milling waves. Blinded by their blinking, those cold white star reflections in the midst of the heat of a summer afternoon. And the onceness of each individual reflection in the myriad of twinkling.

THE STAR OF THE SEA

BEFORE our very eyes they changed. There was a shimmer on the sea, the white metallic lustre of sun dissolved by high cloud, and it flecked and flickered all the while they were filming. From where we were watching they were a long way back because the tide had gone out so very far; the cameras and gantries were stark silhouettes and the figures Lowry-like pin men. The whole scene had an undulating movement to it as though we were watching a mirage or a scene in a heat haze – one moment a figure would be there, then it would be suspended, then replicate itself, flick from tin to lead in a wink. The scene held itself, pulsating gently against a nudging wind, saturated in silence.

Only days ago the cars and Landrovers had arrived and then the bus with the ladies. They tumbled out in a flurry of permanent waves, merry hats, golden legs, and twinkling eyes. I'd not known why they had come and asked Aunty May. She was one of the best informed in the butcher's queue and what could not be learned there was soon gleaned from a few minutes in the post office stocking up with penny stamps or letter cards should she want to drop a line to her sister Annie. She knew of course – a group of people from one of the big cities, London she thought it was, were making some kind of film down here.

But why here, I wanted to know, anxious to glean the virtue of this town that the smart people from London knew about but that as yet had left me untouched.

Why here?

There was nothing for it but to hang around and find out. I was quite good at this. I'd learnt it because I'd had to. Old Ned was better. He gazed absently at the horizon with his blue eyes matching the sapphire of the sea, whilst people poured confidences into his ears, thinking he was thinking all the time of something else. His non-committal 'oh, ahs' invited proof of more plausibility and accordingly explanations and excuses often followed the tales.

So he had had all the information already – and more – by the time I got to report to him.

"I know," he countered.

"But why here?" I insisted.

"Well, as I understand it, they want the cove round yonder and a beach that's hard facing due east south east so that when the sun comes up everything is in the right place – for the filming," he added.

"Is that all?" I said.

" 'S enough in'it?" he asked.

"Ain't there nowhere else like that but here?"

" 'Ere and near enough London."

"Are they from London?"

"Some *part* of London," which pulled them down only a few notches in their godly ranks.

They obviously had some time to spare and were determined to see the sights and enjoy the vacation. We took them on a trip across the bay; or was it round to Tilly Whim? The girls laughed and giggled as they tottered onto the wave-lurching boat. I gallantly offered my hand as Ned had taught me, steadying them and keeping the boat trim at the same time. As when they arrived there was a tumble of polka dot chiffon, black spots on white, and the shrugging of padded shoulders whilst the giggling took hold. And hands clasped hats which the breeze threatened to toss into the sea.

Above the giggles the gulls added a strident descant as the boat set forth steadily on the gentle swell.

They were all beautiful; dimpled and blonde with lips like cupids bows, succulently outlined in red. One of them had a silly hat perched on her cheeky head with a tiny spotted veil before her eyes. She watched the sea anxiously.

"We're quite safe ma'am," I volunteered.

"I hope so," she smiled in reply, "I've never been in a boat before."

"We carry life jackets."

"Do they really save you're life?"

"They hold you up in the sea," I explained.

"But don't tow you into the shore?" she frowned.

"Oh, no."

"I'm afraid they'd have to do that to save my life," she said gravely. "Haul me right back to the beach."

"Maybe they'll invent those next," I tried to say comfortingly.

"Ah, by then it may be too late," she said wistfully.

"Stella, stop teasing the boy," one of her companions chipped in.

And Stella's sea-green eyes lost the deep emerald of concern and became sun-dappled again with laughter.

"How strange it must seem to you, who have lived all your life on boats to see land lubbers like us," she said merrily. "Do an awful lot of people get sea sick?"

"Only a few – and anyway – I used once to feel queazy."

With this confidence she had conquered me, and my adoration flowed gently out like the creamy wake of the boat we were all in. A keel-hauling might have been gentler, as reality gave way to fantasy. My nights were no longer easy and my appetite failed.

Ned gave me his broad wink and retied the painter as the little throng jostled and tottered away down the quay and back to their places in the town. "Stella," I breathed. "Miss Moris to you," Ned said.

I lurked behind lobster pots and made posies of sea thrift and lavender. I loitered and lingered – watching always for

Stella. There were painful moments when the lurch and toss of the sea seemed to be the movements of my gut when I caught sight of her. Exquisite, breathless, drowning pain.

Ned was able to go into bars – this gained him an advantage and more information: their stay depended on the weather and the tide; they had to get it in the can in three days. The phrases needed unravelling and I struggled with a new vocabulary. They were priestesses and votaresses of the Minoan queen Pasiphae. I spent a day in the library after that – Ned had great trouble getting it straight and I had to look up a lot in a dictionary. Then a bull should rise from the sea – they would create a wave disturbance – but that would be back projected. I struggled through my crash course in mythology and cinematic technique. Mostly I was mystified, but I was ever drugged by my doses of Stella. A day without seeing her produced an agony of withdrawal symptoms.

The season had barely begun; there were few customers for our trips. I gazed moodily into the pools and tore bladder-wrack angrily from rocks. One day I caught her with a friend cautiously dipping a toe into the oily swirling water, two pairs of high heeled shoes left cast up on the beach. They talked quietly to themselves and gently paddled, systematically seriously back and forth along a few feet of sand.

I wished the weather and the tide would not be right.

I dreamt of Stella, like a mermaid rising out of the sea and leaning forward, green wet tresses still sticking to her face while she pressed pale green lips to my pink and soft mouth. I saw myself a mighty bull like Jupiter (for I now knew of the way he captured the nymph, Europa) surging towards her and in the very midst of the filming carrying her away from her dancing figure to a place afar, for me and myself.

"Why look," she said, "Phyl, look."

47

And my head rose cautiously over an upturned dinghy, while the tide crept balefully at my sandals.

Her companion looked.

Stella had gathered some mussels from the sea wall, where the knots of old boat rings had wept red misty tears down the uneven stones.

"They're mussels."

"Are they?" said Phyl, unimpressed.

"They've fallen or been pulled from the wall – I suppose they must be covered when the tide is up."

"Oh, leave them Stel, they're not very nice."

"Oh," she was paying Phyl no attention, "and some of them have been crushed – or at least opened."

"No."

"Perhaps they open when they die." She looked up quickly, she saw me. "Hey, you'll know. Do they open when they die?"

"Mm," I assumed an air of worldly wisdom – anything to stop my face flaming and flaring. "I think so."

"Come and look." Stella proffered them to me. I approached slowly – lest she should hear too quickly the dreadful hammering noise that was emanating from me and blocking my ears.

"Oh!" she gasped. Phyl and I drew closer together.

"Look – there are little pearls inside."

"Oh yes," I said. "Mussels give pearls too – not just oysters."

"Aren't they beautiful?" said Phyl, panting a little. "You could have them made into little earrings."

"Right you are," said Stella, "and look; these two are almost absolutely identical – what a marvellous find."

"Better souvenir from the seaside than a stick of rock. And look, a tiny black one – would you like it, Phyl?"

"Ugh, no," Phyl shuddered. "I don't like the look of it at all. It's quite sinister."

"They're worth more if they are black," I helped.

"It's not the value – they've come free anyway –"

"Gifts from the sea," Stella sighed. "Here – you have it – keep it for luck!"

I hesitated.

"Would you like it?"

"Oh, yes please."

"There – a souvenir of us – for you by the sea."

"That's a sort of backwards present," she added. I laughed. She laughed with me and she put her forefinger on my nose while my ears lit up.

I wished the weather and tide would never be right.

But they were. We saw them one day – the girls muffled by coats but dressed in flaring robes nevertheless, making their way across the sand. Leaving little black pools behind them, making one pattern and then another, forming and reshaping, whilst Jeeps and Landrovers and other vehicles jerked and trundled and squandered around the shoreline. They stopped and started: sometimes small figures broke away from clusters and then rejoined or made yet another cluster. All day long I watched them and Aunty May was furious; I'd missed all my meals.

The magic lantern flickered, the figures guttered and sighed and were extinguished by wave light. I could barely make it out. I screwed up my eyes. The atmosphere faltered so heavily between us like the robes of time – the dancers were as removed from my sight as the nymphs they portrayed were from my experience. And yet they were there and I felt the tugging of their prayers and the keening of their gestures. The iridescent masque spawned its entreaty into the sand, into the waves, up to the sky and out out out to the depths of the silvery sea.

I could feel the emerald eyes of that beautiful girl urging some surging god from the emerald expanse – and yet it was all spattered on a sheet of silver – so that as the effect they wanted from the waves started working, I saw great silver plumes of water breaking and splintering and thundering along the foam-flecked waves. The double vision recurred and between the glinting figures, I thought there was a foam flecked horse – but hadn't they meant a bull? – and a flying white mane and a thunder of hoofs whilst one figure seemed to fly towards its white creaminess and there was a shout and a scattering of pearls and a triumphant whinny; then vision clicked back into single again and the figures were looking at each other, gesturing, shrugging, then running and shouting. One figure bent down and picked up something – and then more crying and running – and eveyone scampered backwards as a freak large wave broke from the silver tapestry and drenched the feet of some of the dancers and wet a few tyres and the cameras.

I think they must have discouraged the event from getting into the news. Ned said it would be bad publicity – and then they went soon after – they had got a second shot in the can – he was quite fluent in the language by now. I caught a glimpse of Phyl as she left, and she showed me what she'd picked up from the beach – another pearl.

"There were others," she said, "but the wave got them too. But look at this one. I prefer white. I'll wear it in memory of Stella."

"Suitable," I said. "Pearls are for sorrow."

"Even black ones?" she said.

"Particularly black ones," I replied.

There was only a little write up in the local paper, mentioning the sad incident of the dancing girl who was swept out to sea, during the filming of a dance sequence for *Daedalus*, a major new film. I didn't think they'd mention her name. I thought the film company would not have let them disclose such information. They need not have worried – the local paper has a penchant for typographical error – they called her Stella Maris. I found out 'Daedalus' made mazes, and gave Aunty May the pearl one Christmas, by which time I'd come out of mourning and had found a new star.

THE LAST HIRING OF THE SEASON

THERE had been the wild spilling on the sea, dashing about in the elegant little motor boat. The laughter and smiles, as the wind and the sun and the sea caressed them all. And then the jerk and the cry and the disappearing. We couldn't believe a disaster like that; all the time we were thinking and acting we were battling with incredulity. I dived over first, and the child's father next. The boat wandered and we had no markers. And we could see nothing; it was murky and dark as though almost deliberately a smoke screen had been put up. Cold, too, much colder than the warm sun above made us believe. The end of the season, the last boat of the holiday – probably the last hiring of all that year.

And they, happy family, all ready to go to take up the reins of the lives they'd left behind. New schools, old friends, old haunts, new games. One more dash across the briny, one more flirtation with the sea. Now this light-heartedness was being derided – no playfellow I – master only.

We hear, we hear – too late.

His brothers screamed to him, screamed to him from the side of the boat, but his ears fast closing with water, closing from the world, were deaf.

I found him bobbing against an anchor, drifting against the rope. His hair lifting and dropping and his limbs light as air making the hypnotic gestures of a dancer in a trance.

I recovered him.

His father helped me put him in the boat, the mother held him in her arms like a new born child. His brothers sat frozen and still, their white faces like ranks of stone saints on the side of a cathedral. Unmoving and sober. I shivered – and I shivered, and then the thunder.

The thunder seemed to grumble deep from the bowels of the earth. Automatically like an animal my heart turned over. My stomach turned to cold water and I felt instinctive fear. The throat tightening, the held breath, the pausing to watch, whilst the senses, sentinels of the body fully alerted scanned, scanned for information. It always signified something deep and uncomfortable in nature. Some unease and dissatisfaction. And there was threatening in the sound. It rolled across the sea, and echoed far, far and away against clouds stacked up monumentally on the horizon. There was a pause.

The mother looked at her drowned son. All I can do for him is love him, she seemed to say, all a mother knows is to love. And if with that cloak and pulling of my heart I could bring him back to me I would. I can love like that until my heart breaks. But I know, and this is my despair, that I cannot manage so great an act of love as that. This is why I cry and why I moan – because I cannot do that. I did all else. I brought him here – but cannot keep him now. My love is useless. Oh God, give me back my son.

And she lifted up the white, limp little hand and let it drop. It fell, so heavy and awkward onto her lap. And the pale dead face had all the dreams fled from it. A deserted playground – vacant and empty. There were no tears; only from the sky, big thunderdrops started to fall.

LADY LAVENDER

AMIDST the precious decor of mint and off-white, the ivory doylies on the tables, the damask napkins rested against fresh flowers and the cake stands. The soft sibilance of discreet conversation webbed the tables like a hair net. There was a comfortable, deep piled thud in the rhythm of crockery against crockery, the rise and fall of murmuring conversation. The scent of lavender water and phlox swam from the tables to the plaster relief ceiling – past the large ornate gold-framed mirror over the mantlepiece.

Outside, against the blue sky, the flags flapped and fluttered, cracking like the slapping of canvas. The white stack of the hotel, vaunting on its haunches, seemed like a great boat, breasting the front like the waves, forever calling serenely with its load of elderly ladies between by-gone days and eternity.

With paper-thin skin, lace at the neck, the heliotrope lady watched herself manipulate the sugar tongs with scrupulous care. The only other single occupant of a table deftly dabbed the area between stiff upper lip and moustache. The pink of his face suited the grey of his suit like an ice cream confection. The chambermaids called him the Strawberry Sorbet and her Miss Heliotrope.

One day he was sitting, chin on hands, and hands resting on head of malacca cane, on the old green overlooking the stone pier. She wandered by in a swirl of purple frills, averted her head a fraction, dipped her head with extreme grace whilst he raised his hat and smiled an affable smile.

Gulley and I, barefoot and hiding under an old boat, nudged each other conspiratorially. We'd sit there and watch the feet of the world passing in front of us.

"Gulley," I said, "I don't think I've seen such a Ladylike lady."

"What, 'er?" he said.

"Of course."

" 'Er?" he said again incredulously.

Then Gulley told me he had seen her feeding a sea serpent at midnight, one night when she didn't think he was watching.

"What with?" I asked scornfully, not really believing him.

"Handfuls of seaweed," he retorted, "pulled from the rocks by the pier."

"You never, Gulley – you ain't telling the truth," I cried.

"If yer don't believe me you cummun wotch."

"What d'yer mean?"

"I mean – wotch 'er, like what I did. Then you'd know, then you'd see."

"Where did you watch her?"

"Down there, down by the little beach."

The little beach was a small stretch of sand between the old pier and where the rocks started. Now folk use it for launching their boats it's hardly large enough to squat in, and at a full tide it's completely covered.

"I dunno if I'd be allowed out."

"Say you're coming to give me a message – about school or something," Gulley said, ever guileful and with a quick appreciation of what was acceptable in the eye of parents.

"I'll try," I muttered. "When?"

"I think it was about eleven."

"Oh! Crumbs –"

"No – I mean yes – I remember it was low tide. No – come at low tide tonight."

"I'll try," I said again, torn between the extreme difficulty of getting away and the promise of Lady Lavender with a sea serpent or, if not, at least the opportunity of jeering at smarty pants Gulley.

The excuse, already lame, took sick and died as the evening wore on. By nightfall deception had taken its place. I retired to bed and then out through the window, down the slates of the scullery and off into the darkness. It was a well-worn route.

The moon was up – but the tattered clouds were obscuring it in a hurried and worried fashion. Gulley was there, his carroty mop gleaming like a tangled bundle of copper wire atop the rock. I skulked quickly from shadow to shadow until I reached him, then panting, crouched beside him. He nudged me.

My stomach turned and dropped. Down the steps, across the briskly manicured lawn, she flowed. Wraith-like, there was no mistaking the cut of the clothes, the shape of the hairstyle, the form of the body. Her pace was neither hurrying nor holding back. It was sure and determined. No meandering. Across the road, up the promenade, past the pier, towards us. Through the rocks, past us, and beyond, down purposefully to the water's edge.

There was no anticipation, no hesitation, no looking round in case of spectators – just across the black velvety smoothness of the night sea a call and ululating yodelling cry that spread out like a wash of curling foam, a flow of surf flying over the waves.

And she stooped and clawed at some glistening bladder-wrack on the rocks. Then from the sea, a disturbance; a dislocation in the smooth pattern of waves. I tell you, from about a hundred yards offshore, a serpentine and craggy head broke the surface of water and rose and rose from the sea. As it grew up towards the sky, so it came nearer and nearer, until suddenly towering over her, it swooped its neck down and towards the Lavender Lady. Her arm looked like the most fragile porcelain, her figure a Meissen statuette, so still and delicate and small by comparison to the large and ugly animal beside her. And she was feeding it seaweed.

"What did I tell yer?" Gulley couldn't resist crowning my incredulity with this triumph. "Yer right," conceding nothing but total defeat. It was a night of unnatural behaviour anyway; I couldn't run against the natural trend of events.

"Is it really just this seaweed?"

"Yer, just this stuff, here." He pulled a bit from the rock, I watched him. When I next looked up it had gone and the little figure by the waveline was delicately picking her way up the beach, holding up her skirts from the puddles that gather in the larger wrinkles left by the sand at low tide.

The following day, down amongst the lobster pots, I caught Gulley already practising. The yodelling noise sounded like an alpenhorn with sinusitis. But we practised. And in the end, I mastered it.

In the meantime the affable smiles and nods between the Lavender Lady and Captain Doesnip continued with many a nudge and wink from Gulley and me.

One day Gulley announced the call was good enough. And he added that there was a low tide too. "But what if she's there too?' I protested.

"She can't be," he said.

"Oh, why not? You've not watched every night."

"She don't do it every night," he said.

"Oh yes," I said. "How do you know?"

"Because some low tides," he said, all cocky, "she's at the bridge tables in the hotel, because I've seen her."

"All right then," I said, "but you still don't know about tonight."

"Yes I do, because they've all gone on a charabanc outing."

"All?"

"Well, all the ladies," he conceded.

"Oh, okay then," I said, "but what'll we do if it

comes?''

"Just give it the seaweed," Gulley said, with awe-inspiring simplicity.

"S'pose it doesn't just want the seaweed?''

"That's all it seems to want.''

"But. . . s'pose –''

"What? You're afraid.''

"No.''

"Well then.''

"Well then what? *You* make the call.''

"You know I can't do it.''

"But I don't know that I want to do it.''

"Not to say you saw it again – that it came for you?''

He knew, because he felt it too, that that was exactly what I wanted to see, to feel, to know. It was an absolutely undisguised opportunity to excercise some awful and dreadul power. For some extraordinary reason it felt like being able to call the winds and the waves, and the storms and the tides to heel. To orchestrate the whole sea symphony. I knew when the noise finally came right that it had in it the extraordinary quality of wildness and madness. It was raw nature, the deep throat call of a woman in labour, the shrill terror of an animal dying in pain. It was raw, naked, aggressive, and savage, but it had power and authority, and it called all these elements into my throat to do my bidding when and how I chose.

I knew I could do it. I knew it was there. (The adult might have been content with knowledge, the child had to see tangible proof.)

"All right then, all right.''

"Good lad.''

"But you have plenty of that seaweed ready, Gulley.''

"Course," he said.

So at low tide we picked our way through the streams of rivulets, wandering back to the sea from the rock pools higher on the beach. Low tide – a spring tide, and a still warm night.

I didn't feel at all frightened. The whole beach seemed so calm and peaceful. The little town with its lights smiled back serenely at me like an indulgent aunt. There was a complete air of utter relaxation.

We meandered up to the water's edge. I placed my feet firmly apart but they had found that soggy kind of sand that sinks into little puddles round your ankles.

"Go on," said Gulley.

I raised my cupped hands to my mouth and called. . . only once. The ringing of it seemed to continue after I'd stopped.

We saw it, we saw the broken ripples, the breaking waters, we saw a rising and heard a flow of the rushing tide. Across the screaming beach a figure ran, a portly, dapper figure, careering up to us. And as he ran he cried out an enormous shouting roll of noise – and the nearer he got to the sea, the larger he seemed to be. I never saw if the sea serpent came or not, I was so busy watching him and Gulley's transfixed, horrified, and angry stare. But who or what horrified and angered him, I couldn't fathom. All I knew was that as the cry died away into a sobbing sibilance and once that was lost on the wind, I'd heard a sound of ultimate authority. Humbled, all the pride fell from my throat.

It was the Captain.

"Don't tamper," he said, softly and briskly, "don't tamper." And we were quiet and abashed.

"Where did you hear that?"

We didn't answer.

"Who taught you to make the noise?" he asked again, this time more gently. The gentleness was more persuasive.

"Miss Lavender," Gulley offered.

"Miss Lavender?" he asked.

"Your lady friend."

"Ah!" he said. "Ah!" – and like a solution long looked for and now discovered, he exhaled.

"And you," he said, looking at me – darkly, sternly but kindly – "to make it you must have merman blood in the veins."

"Sir?"

"Ha!" his laughter was a shout of sudden joy and relief. And then serious, very serious.

"You leave the sea serpents to Miss Lavender – they only eat the flowers from her garden – I don't think they really like little boys."

"Would it have eaten us?"

"It? It? My lad, they were on their way, all of them that could hear would have arrived after that call! Not only. . . What did you call her? Miss Lavender?!"

He sat down suddenly on a rock; and then turned and said quickly "I must go, I expect the ladies will be returning. Perhaps you should get back before your parents miss you – I should hate them to know where you are – let alone what you were up to."

When the courtship had been accepted and had run its course, and looked as though the union might be permanent, we ventured to talk to Captain Doesnip.

"Good news, eh lads?" he said in his brisk manner.

"What's that, sir?"

"Lady Lavender, as you call her, has accepted me."

"You mean you will be getting married?"

"That's about the sum of it."

"When?"

"Soon enough, soon enough me boy."

Manners retrieved the conversation. There seemed very little to say. The young cannot see any good reason in older people marrying.

"Congratulations to you both."

"Thank you, Gulley, thanks."

"Was it the sea serpent that decided you?" I asked.

"Sea serpent?" he asked looking unseeingly out at the horizon.

"– Ehrm, well –"

He broke in: "I know you call her Lady Lavender but I call her my nereid. D'you know what that is?"

"No, sir."

"Sea nymph, lad, nymph of the sea.'

"*Your* sea nymph?" said Gulley.

"Mine, Gulley."

"Like you're her boss, the king of the sea?"

"Something like that," he twinkled, with eyes of ultramarine.

"I might never have found her, had you two not been so useful. She's taken plenty of finding. But then she's a jewel of great worth. Would you believe how long I've looked?"

He stopped talking and looked up, as though interrupted by a thought or idea. Then quickly he smiled and looked at us both. He reached into his upper pocket and drew out his pocket handkerchief. There was an electric flash of blue like a kingfisher's wing, and a searing crack of static. My ears suddenly filled with a dreadful whirring sound.

Before everything became completely black, whilst the cloud of oblivion hovered round the edges of my vision, this message ran loudly into my head:

"Gulley has forgotten. Lady Lavender and I will be untraceable. No one will remember us – and least of all believe a small boy who sees sea serpents. But this I won't take from you, which by right of your sea-ancestry is yours."

Then the crash that was either all the roaring in my ears reaching the ultimate climax, or my body falling to the ground.

Gulley's copper knob extinguished the sun. I had

remembered. He hadn't. Subsequent discreet enquiries drew complete blanks. And who does believe small boys who tell tales about sea serpents? Do you? ? ?

TOBY AND THE CRAB-LINES

M R Goodyear was wheeled out and wheeled in. Every day when the weather was good like the fine day lady in the weatherhouse, out he came. Every day when the weather was bad, like the lady he was in. In and out. Out and in. Life was simple. In when it was cold and out when it was warm. Cold in, warm out. Simple. Cut and dried. Simple like old age, that's cut and dried; out, in, being cut off from the flow of life and vigour: the cells no longer regenerate; like cut flowers they are dying on the stem.

Cut off, from the life source, very removed from the life source when one is old.

And dried. Dried like an old poppy seed case, the browned stems of late summer. Dried in the sun, fishes turned to stick by the heat, fragile and brittle.

Cut and dried.

And on a really clement day and with the goodwill and availability of one of the staff he would be wheeled to the old quarry quay. Along the line where the donkey engines jostled with their trucks of rough-hewn, white dusty stone down to the old quayside. Here the scents and sounds of the sea coupled with the sight of children fishing sent Mr Goodyear into a comfortable haze of happy witness and warm reminiscence.

His eyes moved to the beach, and settled waterily on the bronze Romeos strutting amongst the colourful sunbathers, squeezed out like stripey toothpaste on the sherbet lemon sand.

Unresisting, abandoned, like deflated balloons. The sunbathers lie collapsed like seals flopped on an ice-floe. Neatly aligned in rows, sun orientated like the heavy heads of sunflowers, heliophiles, every man jack of them. Limbs heavy with sunshine, the golden bodies move slowly, swimming through treacle. The knee-deep rich honey-thick beach oozes the holiday hours away alongside the docile and placid sea.

Back on the quay the breeze is smart, and the sea-gulls scream and wheel in the blue sky overhead. A white-haired little boy crouches over his crabline, and earnestly baits it with bacon rind. When he stands his thin incurving calves and prominent knees give his legs a curiously buckled jockeyish look. He concentrates, winces; he's pricked his finger on the hook.

His brothers come up to him. "What you doing Toby?"

"Tryin' to do this."

"What's wrong?"

"I pricked my finger on the hook. Look!"

"Tut. You would, wouldn't you, Tobe?"

"Come, let me help."

"No, I'll do it myself."

"I only offered."

"Oh all right then, go on.'

"You caught anything yet?"

"NO," defiantly.

"I'm not surprised with this thing."

"I know."

"Well what you gonna do about it?"

Shrugs shoulders.

"Why don't you get some decent bait?"

"No money."

"Why not?"

"Where's your pocket money?"

"I spent it all in Playland."

"Oh Toby, you would."

He gives a conspiratorial grin, watches what his elder brother is doing, deftly twisting the hook through the rind, and then paying out the line ready to cast, one foot on the

63

end of the line, steadying it and preventing that too being hurled into the sea.

"Watch, Toby."

He watches; glancing as the line arcs elegantly and plops into the water alongside the other half dozen that the fishes ignore with a dumb arrogance.

He's lying down on his tummy, watching the sea bobbing against the old wall; occasionally directing operations to fellow anglers when the opportunity presents itself.

"I see a crab there."

"Where?" the surprised lad to his right asks.

"There by that big stone."

"Yes, I've got it, you're right."

"Course I am," a mock swagger.

"Carefully. . . up. . . oh you've lost him."

A splash. The recast and new hope: the freshly dealt cards.

Behind him on the quay, an old man can't help chuckling. And more so. Toby stands. His small nose tips up insolently making his face even more innocent and babyish than it really is. He concentrates, frowning slightly, his blond thatch low over his brow. The lapping of the waves increases to a licking and a slapping sound as old Ned brings in his boat and all the lines on that side of the quay are drawn up. . . his with them. He carefully unravels some of the knots in his line, hums a little to himself, totally absorbed. The gulls screech and wheel away into the wide blue sky.

Time to recast. A swing and a throw and away soars the line and hook and sinker, and then the tug and the scramble. . . and too late. Without the steadying foot the weight has proved too effective and all Toby's line has disappeared from view. He looks round quickly and anxiously. But his brothers have gone. He has to help himself and rescue the line.

Camaraderie prevails. The earlier assisted angler effects a complicated rescue operation. Much gratitude is expressed. Amidst dimples and thanks, he casts again. This time with great attention to the mooring on dry land of his line.

Mr Goodyear, the old gentleman, watches the lines unravel. Growing older, he thinks to himself, unfolds its own truths.

We slowly become aware that there is only one direction in living. As children the choices of routes seem numerous and various and interchangeable; the older we get, the less roads we know we are going to travel. We have already made choices that have determined the way. Often we have made decisions unwittingly, that have quite precluded the taking of thousands of others.

Although we live in hope, we begin to see that to stake all on tomorrow is not to make the most of today. When we learn to be totally absorbed by 'now' we begin to have a tangible grasp on eternity.

Toby immersed in his crablines, his refusal even to contemplate a change of bait had reached a compromise with the future and a balance with the present. An enviable position between what is now but what will never be.

Lap, lap, lap. . .

Mesmerised by the flow of light caustics, half asleep on his crooked arm, the little white head lies heavy on his elbow. He is contemplating everything and nothing. The fine wrinkles of light across the sand on the sea bed, doubled and trebled like a lace net of light, are perpetually moving and dodging and evading permanency.

There's a slight scuffle. One of the anglers shifts position. His neighbour's attention is caught. Suddenly they are all alerted. Toby screws round on his seat; their own lines forgotten now, abandoned, dangle lazily, anywhere. All concentrate on landing the fellow fisher's crab.

One runs up with a bucket. His mate carefully lowers a net. Hanging by one greedy pincer the cumbersome crab is hauled gently upwards. His determination not to leave the succulent bait is his undoing. All seven other legs are wildly waving in the unnatural air, seeking purchase but bringing no rescue. A slowly-lowered net settles below the uncouth clawing prey. The giddy and precarious ascent continues. The quay holds its breath, the gulls freeze in their flight. One more wild cancerian scrabble, the hold is lost; it falls; it is caught; swiftly pulled upwards; splashed into a bucket.

Exhalation.

Exultation.

Suddenly the sounds of the rest of the beach, previously held at bay, flood over the conspiracy of anglers. The watchers pass on, the sunbathers resettle, the guillemots squawk, and the motorboats in the bay commence a-throbbing.

Toby sidles up and looks. Dark and menacing, the large crab lies sulking in the darkest part of the bucket.

"What are you going to do with it?"

"Chuck it back."

"Yes, best thing," he agrees. Shrugs and slowly winds in his still knotty line.

A small sigh, the puckered attention to detail, a glance at the outside world and out goes the line again, singing through the air like a bird of paradise.

There's no magic to enchantment. And enchantment is never-ending.